To —
My Best wishes
Russell Abt

A BoxCar full of love
Health and Happiness
for you and yours

Fontana

Charlotte —
Old time —
some of the best
Elmer

Elma, Born in a Boxcar

by

Robert G. O'Briant

authorHOUSE™

1663 LIBERTY DRIVE, SUITE 200
BLOOMINGTON, INDIANA 47403
(800) 839-8640
WWW.AUTHORHOUSE.COM

First published by AuthorHouse 12/09/05

ISBN: 1-4208-8731-9 (sc)

Printed in the United States of America
Bloomington, Indiana

This book is printed on acid-free paper.

TABLE OF CONTENTS

To Jim and Linda

ACKNOWLEDGEMENTS

There are many people to whom I am grateful. My wife, Pauline, heads the list. She edited the entire manuscript, rewrote, and made suggestions along the way. In addition, she helped keep me focused when I veered off course. Her support and encouragement made this book happen.

I appreciate the assistance of Wilma Birks who tracked down the pictures of Mound House through the Nevada State Railroad Museum and the Nevada Historical Society.

I am profoundly grateful to Lee Philip Brumbaugh, curator of photography at the Nevada Historical Society and his outstanding staff, Marta Gonzalez Collins and docent Richard Cruz who all patiently sought out the photos in the archives of Nevada history.

Jane O'Cain, History Curator and Collections Manager of the Nevada State Railroad Museum, was helpful in retrieving pictures of Mound House and articles of interest in addition to providing valuable counsel for further research.

I thank Louise and Peter Dolcini, two of my dearest and most literate friends, for proof reading the manuscript and making constructive suggestions. After suggesting the addition of a number of punctuation marks, they dubbed themselves, "The King and Queen of Commas."

A special thanks to Robert Fontana, one of Nevada's finest and most versatile artists, for the book cover design. He has developed his own unique art form. As a multi-talented artist combining traditional art forms and his skills as a silver engraver, he hand engraves on color-coated aluminum. This becomes a "metal canvas" on which he scratches and gouges to produce masterpieces. He is one of the most talented men I have ever known.

He is 85 years old and works every day creating some of Nevada's finest art.

Finally, I want to thank the subject of this story, Elma Smalley. She has been patient, tolerating my probing inquires during the last year. We spent countless hours together during interviews and many more hours on the telephone recalling her remarkable life and transferring the events from her memory to the written word.

INTRODUCTION

I have been asked, "Why did you want to write a book about Elma?" The answer is simple. She's a storyteller and has many tales to tell. How often have you met a lady who was born in a boxcar, rode a horse to a one-room school to teach in rural Nevada, built her own house, drove a locomotive at age six, and drove her grandmother in a 1928 Dodge, 130 miles from Reno, Nevada to Sacramento, California at age twelve? And that's just for openers.

Seldom do you have the opportunity to know a person like Elma Smalley. She is nearly ninety years old now and has been in a wheelchair for the last several years. She had to stop driving her car in 2004 and that restriction curbed her activities because she is a traveler at heart.

She would be on the road today if she could walk and drive. However, she still plays bridge with her bridge group, goes out to dinner, and rents a house every summer at Lake Tahoe, Bodega Bay, or Graegle to spend time away from Reno with her friends and family.

Several years ago, my wife Pauline invited her cousin Wilma Birks, and Elma, a lifelong friend, to spend a week with us in Hawaii. It was during this vacation I first heard the stories of Elma's life. We are both early risers and over coffee at 5:00 A.M. we would talk. Actually, she would talk and I would listen to the incredible stories of Nevada and her life experiences. It was then I decided that these stories had to be preserved.

Elma and I have spent hours together on the telephone and in person during the writing of this book and I have never heard her complain about anything. I know she is in pain most of the time, but when I inquire about her health, the answer is always, "I'm doing pretty good, how are you?" Her attitude is contagious. You feel uplifted when you're with a positive person and she is positive plus. It has been a privilege to know and work with her during the writing of this book. She told the stories and I wrote them as she related them. Thank you Elma for all your patience.

BEGINNINGS

I was born in a boxcar, March 7, 1916 in Mound House, Nevada, a small town located between Carson City and Dayton. I entered this world with the assistance of Doctor Gerow, a physician who drove the seven miles from Carson City.

Mound house was the site of a large gypsum mine as well as a railroad terminal, where the Southern Pacific met the Virginia-Truckee. My father, James Alvin May, was a conductor on the S.P. His route was between Mound House and Wabuska, and he made the round trip daily. My mother, Amy Eliza Harling, was from Derby Dam, Nevada where her father was employed as a member of the crew building an irrigation dam on the Truckee River. It was located approximately twenty miles east of Sparks, a large railroad terminal. Dad was working out of there at the time, where he had a run east to Wadsworth. He met my mother on a Saturday night at a dance in Wadsworth and from that time forward an incredible courtship began. When Amy knew Jim's train was coming through Derby Dam, she would stand along the tracks and he would throw her love notes. One day she received a note informing her he wanted to give her an engagement ring and he would leave it at the station in Wadsworth. So Mom got on her horse, rode to Wadsworth and later that day became the future Mrs. James Alvin May. Her brothers were dubious about the whole affair and teased her, saying that the ring was probably a rhinestone, and the only way to prove it was a real diamond was to see if it would cut glass. And so on a window at their home in Derby Dam they scratched the letters AMY. (A few years back my son Jim was attending the University of Nevada where he was involved in a research project about irrigation. He went to Derby Dam to look the place over, and there, three quarters of a century later, still etched in the window of the little house where my mother once lived, were the letters AMY.) Mom and Dad subsequently married in Sparks and produced three offspring: Jim was first, Margaret came two years later, and I arrived five years after Margaret.

To say our home was merely an empty boxcar is misleading. It was actually three cars joined together with full-length leather flaps. The cars were older ones that had been retired and taken out of service by the railroad. They were placed on wooden platforms and remodeled with interior walls and doors. Because our little home was located about twenty feet from the main track, it shook like the San Francisco earthquake whenever the Wabuska train went by.

The first car was our kitchen and dining room, the second, our parents' bedroom, the third, the children's bedroom. We had the luxury of a water supply in the kitchen, but the bathroom was an outhouse behind the cars. We felt privileged to have such upscale housing because the brakemen had only two boxcars and the work crews shared a single one. Other employees lived in little yellow company houses, tiny one-room units, much too small to accommodate a family.

I started school in Mound House and what a joy it was being one of the "railroad children!" We led a unique existence. For example, every New Year's Eve, we would decorate the locomotive, climb aboard for a trip to Dayton, and blow the whistle all the way, seven miles. What fun it was!

Another amusing activity was riding the cowcatcher as the train returned to Mound House. The locomotive was equipped with a cowcatcher, a large iron wedge-shaped device mounted on the front of the engine designed to deflect cattle standing on or near the tracks. We would wait for the train on its final approach and jump on the cowcatcher for the ride into town.

One of the most exciting experiences I ever had as a child occurred one day when I accompanied Dad to the gypsum mine, which was up a mountain west of town, where he had a meeting with the foreman. When they finished their business, the foreman asked if I'd like to have a ride down the mountain. Always eager for a new adventure, I jumped at the chance and Dad assented. The ride was to be in an ore bucket which transported gypsum from the mine to the processing plant, a distance of three miles. The "bucket" was actually an aerial tram, much like a present day ski lift. After explaining I'd have to hang on tight, he said, "One more thing, I'll have to call down and tell them to stop the bucket so you don't get dumped with the gypsum crystals." That was even more fun than the cowcatcher.

When I think about the freedom and experiences we had, I doubt that many of the things we did could happen in today's world. Can you imagine New Year's Eve with a Southern Pacific locomotive, decorated with banners and streamers, chugging down the tracks through the desert with children hanging off the sides, blowing the whistle and singing at the tops of their voices? Or a locomotive coming into town with four or five kids sitting on the cowcatcher? Or a six-year-old riding an ore bucket down the mountain and having the plant come to a halt so she could get off? I don't think so. We did things that can never be relived. Nevada was still the Wild West, and I consider myself fortunate to have grown up while it was untamed and unspoiled.

SCHOOL

I started school in Mound House when I was six. The school was an old square building located in a large arid field with nothing around it—no trees, no shrubs, no flowers, not any form of landscaping; neither did the school have electricity or indoor plumbing. The only other structure on the property was the outhouse, located in back. The school building sat on a high foundation with steep steps leading from the ground up to a porch and front entrance. We entered the school through a cloakroom where we hung our coats and stored our lunch pails. A large wood-burning stove was in the center of the room. Each student had his or her own desk, assigned by the teacher at the beginning of the school year. Each desk had an inkwell and a large flat writing surface which was hinged at the top and could be raised to provide storage for paper, pencils and books. The oak desk appeared old because of the cracked varnish and initials that had been carved into the writing surface by former students over the years. No one ever carved their last names, only initials and first names. Many of the engravings were inscriptions like "John + Mary", enclosed in a heart pierced by Cupid's arrow.

My first grade teacher was Nancy Jefferson, the daughter of a wealthy family in Kentucky. She had come out west to escape her privileged upbringing and have some fun in the land of sagebrush and cowboys. She was young and extremely attractive, her clothes fashionable and expensive. The school children were impressed with this beautiful, sophisticated young lady. The Mound House School District built special houses for the teachers so they didn't have to live in boxcars. Nancy Jefferson lived in one of these, but she became very fond of my mother and ate dinner at our house many evenings. Mother told me later that she didn't think Miss Jefferson could cook and probably never had to take care of herself before she came to Mound House.

The school was situated halfway between Mound House and the gypsum plant which was located three miles from town. We walked the mile-and-a-half twice daily along the tracks, a direct route to the school. The problem with this path was that it was the habitat of the dreaded local pest, the rattlesnake. The crushed rock railroad bed, metal rails, and tar soaked wooden ties, all absorbed and retained heat, affording the snakes a warm environment. In the springtime the reptiles would crawl up off the cold desert floor and snuggle along the man-made structures which provided them warmth and shelter. Periodically, the men would have a rattlesnake hunt, walking down the railroad tracks to the school killing the snakes along the way. I don't recall anyone getting bitten, but the serpents were always a concern to our parents. Even though Mound House was an area infested with such critters, we, as children, never considered them a deterrent. We played, romping through the fields and open spaces with little concern and left our parents to worry about the potentially deadly creatures.

SHOW AND TELL

Mound House was a railroad town, but unlike most railroad towns because the train didn't go through the town to another destination. When a train came to Mound House it had to stop, turn around and go back on the same track. Although the engines could run backward, they were designed to run forward with the hitch at the rear and a cowcatcher in front. The way the locomotives were turned around was on a section of track called a turntable. The freight and passenger cars could be diverted on sidetracks and pulled in either direction, but the locomotive had to be turned and headed back in the direction whence it came.

The turntable was a large pit about three feet deep with circular mini-tracks on the floor of the pit extending around the circumference. A sturdy steel platform, slightly wider than a locomotive, with a single set of railroad tracks extended across the diameter of the pit. The platform had wheels on each end that rolled on the mini-tracks around the inner circumference of the pit. The railroad tracks leading to the turntable were at ground level and it could be turned into position allowing the engine to drive onto the steel structure. Six men could then walk around the perimeter of the turntable pit pushing the locomotive so that it could be rotated 180 degrees and headed back in the opposite direction on the same track.

The turntable was located between our home and the school. We walked by it every day on the way to school and were fascinated when we could watch the men turn a locomotive around on the huge platform. One morning when I was in the second grade, I was walking to school with several of my schoolmates when we heard a commotion coming from the direction of the turntable and saw a group of men gathered along its perimeter. One man was lying on the ground obviously injured. Several others were huddled around him and everyone seemed very upset. My classmates went on to school, but I was curious, so I proceeded toward the crowd to see what the excitement was about. I walked around the outside of the turntable and crossed a set of tracks and a switching mechanism where an engine could be diverted to a siding. As I crossed the tracks I noticed a man's high-top boot wedged in the switching device. I walked a few steps, but something else caught my eye, so I stopped and looked back. The top of the boot was bloody. I walked over, picked it up, then realized it had a foot in it. Apparently the man had stepped into the switching mechanism as the turntable was moving severing his foot above the ankle. I dropped the boot and ran toward the group surrounding the injured man. I didn't know if I should tell someone about the grisly find. I guessed they already knew because his foot was gone and there was no way to put it back on. I watched as some of the men tried to comfort him and others applied a tourniquet around his leg to stop the bleeding.

I became fascinated with the first-aid process and caught up in the excitement and confusion of the moment when I suddenly realized I was late for school. Our second grade teacher, Sadie Sullivan, was very strict about tardiness. One had to have a good excuse for being late or face the consequences. I thought a serious accident like this was a justifiable excuse, and to prove it I decided to take the boot with its contents to school and offer it to Miss Sullivan as evidence. No one was paying any attention to me, so I walked back to the siding and picked up the boot. I didn't want to get blood on myself so I untied it and carried my tardy excuse by its laces.

When I walked into the schoolroom Miss Sullivan said, "Elma, why are you late?"

I replied, "Miss Sullivan, there was a terrible accident. A man got his leg caught in the turntable and got his foot cut off." I held up the boot and the bloody stump so she could see it and said, "See."

Miss Sullivan gasped and screamed, "Oh my God." After she caught her breath she looked directly into my eyes, obviously avoiding eye contact with the boot, and said quietly, "Elma, get that thing out of this school!" I walked out into the schoolyard and really didn't know what to do with the foot, so I carried it out into the desert where I deposited it behind some sagebrush. I couldn't understand why Miss Sullivan was so angry and upset with me. I just wanted her to know why I was late to school.

ELMA, THE ENGINEER

I used to watch the train come into the station at Mound House from Wabuska, and always focused my attention on the engineer sitting at the controls of that gigantic locomotive pulling all those cars. To me, he represented ultimate power and authority. I knew that my father, as a conductor, had authority and responsibly, but somehow, it seemed to me, the engineer was the number one person.

My father dealt with the passengers and the total operation of the railroad, and I knew that a train could not function without a conductor, but somehow the engineer's job seemed glamorous, steering that magnificent iron monster down the tracks, blowing the whistle at every crossing and capturing the attention of everyone when the train pulled into the station. He would often give a slow wave of his hand to the people waiting on the platform as he slowed the train as it entered the station. Young boys never said, "I want to work for the railroad when I grow up." Instead they said, "I want to be an engineer."

When I was six years old, I asked my father if it might be possible for me to ride in the engine on one of the runs to Wabuska. What I really wanted was to drive the train. Dad knew me well enough to know I had an ulterior motive for wanting to ride in the engine so he promised to ask his friend, the engineer, if it would be all right. Unbeknownst to me, he and the engineer agreed that I could sit at the controls and actually drive the train, so the evening before the ride Dad asked, "Elma, do you think you could drive a train?"

"I guess so," I stammered, innocently.

"Then we'd better have some lessons," he said. So Dad and I sat down that evening and planned our strategy. He explained that uphill grades and flat terrain are not problems. The trick in running a train is to know when and how to apply brakes when the train starts downhill. The enormous weight of a locomotive and the cars it is pulling, without proper restraints, could accelerate to dangerous speeds when descending mountain passes and steep declines and end up a pile of scrap metal at the bottom of a canyon. Thus, we worked out a signal. When he raised his index finger, I was to apply the brakes. When he lowered it, I was to release them.

The morning of the trip to Wabuska arrived and Dad took me along and lifted me into the engine. Of course, the engineer was unaware of our private "code", so when we started down the first grade, he became very tense and anxious. Then I saw Dad's finger rise, and I applied the brakes, and immediately sensed that the engineer relaxed, at least a little, but we still had a long trip with me at the controls. After that, every downhill grade was orchestrated magnificently with the rise of a finger. We made the trip without incident; however, I turned the controls back to the engineer prior to our arrival in Wabuska. We all agreed it would not be prudent for the locals to see a six-year-old girl at the controls of a Southern Pacific locomotive.

I heard the engineer say to my dad, "The girl's a genius. I'm really impressed how she slowed the train on those downhill grades."

My dad replied, "Yes, she is quite a girl."

I've never told anyone about the code though, until now.

MY EASTER BONNET

One Easter season, my father had an unexpected visitor from Salt Lake City. He came from the district office to inspect and evaluate the train's operation from Mound House to Wabuska, but it was actually an evaluation of my father and the administrative personnel responsible for the operation of that particular route. The inspector's assignment required him to make the round trip on the train to insure the railroad's procedures and policies were being followed properly.

I was out of school for the Easter vacation and my father asked me if I would like to ride the train to Wabuska. I was delighted. My parents had bought me a new Easter outfit that I decided to wear on this trip. The dress was white with blue trim around the collar; the hat was made of straw, with a wide brim trimmed in blue with a ribbon that extended halfway down my back. I boarded the train with my father and the inspector and took my seat while they walked through the coaches, talked, and filled out forms fastened to a clipboard. The train consisted of a locomotive, two baggage cars, and one coach car for passengers. The coach car had a large rear platform for passenger viewing and was also used by politicians giving speeches on whistle-stop campaigns. The trip to Wabuska was uneventful. I had a window seat and enjoyed the view of the desert on this clear crisp day as the train made its way through the valleys and over the hills.

On our return trip, I was standing with my father and inspector on the rear platform. As the train slowed on the long steep uphill grade into Mound House, a sudden gust of wind caught the brim of my hat and hurled if off my head down the tracks. I screamed, "Oh no!" and without hesitation, ran into the coach, jumped up on my seat and grabbed the emergency cord strung along the side of the coach. My Dad had instructed me that in an emergency I should pull the cord twice. That's exactly what I did. The train jerked forward and came to a complete stop. I ran back to the platform, jumped off the train and scurried down the tracks in pursuit of my Easter bonnet. After retrieving it, I climbed aboard the train on the rear platform and proceeded down the aisle of the coach to my seat. As I returned, I saw my father and the inspector standing at the far end of the coach looking directly at me. I knew my dad was furious, but the inspector was grinning. He thought the whole incident was amusing.

I think my Dad's evaluation was good. He didn't tell my mother about the hat incident and the only thing he said to me was, "It might be cheaper to buy a new hat than to stop a passenger train."

THE SCHOOL OUTHOUSE

The outhouse was located about thirty yards behind the school. It was a two-hole facility, with little ventilation, designed to conserve warmth in the winter. It was unisex, equipped with toilet paper and an inside lock, the only amenities in this adjunct to our education.

During class, we had to obtain permission from the teacher to leave and use the outhouse. However, before school, during recess, and after school, the facility was available on a first come, first served basis.

One morning when I was in the second grade, I had to use the outhouse before school. I placed my books between the holes but as I shifted to get off the toilet, I bumped the books and they went into the other hole. I was panicked. School was going to start in a few minutes. I knew my teacher, Sadie Sullivan, would be furious if I came to school without my books. It occurred to me that strange things happened to me and I was always in a little trouble and didn't know why. Anyway, I ran into the schoolyard and found my sister and quickly explained my dilemma. She was five years older and very creative. Without hesitation, she suggested we lower someone into the pit to retrieve the books. "I can't fit through the hole," I said. "I'm too big."

She thought for a moment, then said, "I know who we can get: skinny Jimmy Schweiss. He's the littlest kid in the school."

So I hurried out on the playground and found him. "Jimmy," I pleaded. "Would you do me a really big favor, pretty please?"

He looked puzzled and said haltingly, "I guess so, Elma. What do you want me to do?"

I directed him to follow me to the outhouse where my sister was waiting. She said, "Jimmy, you've got to help us. Elma dropped her books down the hole and we need someone to get them out. And you're the only one who'll fit."

He looked aghast. "You mean go down where all that poop is? I don't want to."

"Jimmy," she went on sweetly. "There's nothing to worry about. Elma and I will hold you by the feet, you grab the books and then we'll pull you up."

He began to run away, but Sis', being twice his size, grabbed him, saying, "Listen Jimmy, either you help us get the books or I'll tell Miss Sullivan that you threw them in."

He was a timid little boy, afraid of girls, but especially afraid to get in trouble with the teacher. And so, the two of us, one holding the left foot and the other the right, lowered Jimmy Schwiess into the pit, head first. All was quiet for a few seconds, then he sputtered, "I've got 'em. Pull me up." How we got him out unscathed, I'll never know, but he came up, retching, eyes watering, handed me the excrement encrusted texts, and ran off to the classroom. I cleaned the books as well as I could with toilet paper, but they were still wet, brown and smelly.

When I got to class, the telltale odor was immediately discerned by Miss Sullivan. She followed her nose to my desk and after I explained what had happened, she ordered me and the books out of the classroom and home to clean up. When I got outside, I threw the books in the sagebrush, then hurried home and told my mother the whole story. I expected her to be upset; instead, she cleaned me up and sent me back to school. I knew she couldn't wait to tell Dad of my misadventure.

On the way out the door she admonished me, "Try not to lose any more books, Elma, and by the way, you bring Jimmy home with you after school, if he'll come, so I can thank him too."

DRIVER'S ED. 101

My father owned the first car in Mound House. It was a 1922 Dodge touring car with white sidewalls. Dad was very proud of it and kept it clean and shiny, which was no small feat in the dusty Nevada desert. Earlier that year, he had ordered a Ford that was delivered by railroad, but he didn't like the starting mechanism, a crank, so he returned it and ordered the Dodge that started by pressing a button.

By the time I was six years old, my most passionate wish was to learn to drive. I pestered Dad until he relented. At first he let me sit on his lap and hold the steering wheel while he backed out of the garage. This was such a thrill I showed up at the garage any time he took the car out for a drive. These mini-driving lessons

24

continued until I was tall enough to reach the pedals when Dad let me sit in the driver's seat and gave me a real lesson. "Elma," he said, "you have watched me for a long time. Now do exactly what you've seen me do." So I depressed the clutch, put the car in low gear, then I let the clutch out. The car lurched forward a couple of feet and promptly died.

"What did I do wrong?" I pleaded.

"Well, you let the clutch out a little too fast," he replied patiently. "Now try it again, but this time let the clutch out very slowly with your left foot, and at the same time, give it the gas gently with your right foot."

I wanted so badly to do it right and impress my dad that I concentrated very hard, followed his instructions explicitly, and lo and behold! it worked. That first day I drove only in low gear around the yard until I had the clutch operation mastered. I felt so smug I thought I was ready to drive to San Francisco, so within days, because of my persistence, Dad taught me to shift and let me drive around town. This was before the days of mandatory drivers' licenses and insurance, and besides, since we owned the only car in town, there was no danger of a two-car accident.

In all those early days of driving, the only mishap I ever had was not inflicted on the car but on me. One day when I was six, someone left the front driver's side door ajar and I didn't notice it. I climbed up on the running board, grabbed the door handle, smacked myself in the face, and broke off my two front teeth. Fortunately, they were baby teeth, and my parents assured me I'd soon have permanent replacements. It was a small price to pay for all the joy I got from driving that 1922 Dodge.

MEMORIES OF A SECOND GRADER

My closest and dearest friend was a classmate named Madeline Frugoli. Her father was the section foreman for the Southern Pacific in Mound House. One of his main responsibilities was to tend the locomotive and keep the fire burning in the firebox. They never let the fire go out because it would take hours to reheat the water that produced steam to power the engine. Madeline's mother was an energetic trim woman who ran the local boarding house. She cooked and provided meals for the single men who worked for the railroad and the Portland Cement Gypsum Mine. The Frugolis' house seemed so big to me, maybe because I lived in the boxcar section of town.

I loved going to their home. It had the largest dining room and the longest table I have ever seen. The table would seat forty men, twenty on each side. The room was long and narrow, providing just enough space for the table and a row of chairs on each side. The most impressive aspect of the room, however, especially to a second grader, was that there was homemade salami hanging from the ceiling of the dining room. At times, seventy-five to one hundred sticks of two-foot long salami dangled from hooks above the table. The room reminded me of pictures of stalactites you could see in Carlsbad Caverns in New Mexico. When they ran out of antipasto at dinner, Mrs. Frugoli would stand up on a chair, unhook a stick of salami, and slice it for her guests. Sometimes, she even gave me a piece.

THE MILK CAN CAPER

In the 1920's Dayton was an active gold mining town. A large dredging operation produced thousands of ounces of gold which was processed and made into 27.5 pound bars, then transported to Reno. The Southern Pacific carried the precious metal from Dayton to Mound House where it was transferred to the V&T for the final leg of its journey to Reno.

Train robberies were prevalent in the twenties, so the method of shipment was tailored to thwart any mischief that might occur from the time the gold left Dayton until it arrived in Reno.

It so happened that there were a number of dairies in the Dayton Valley that also shipped milk to Reno by rail. Someone had the great idea that the gold bars could be disguised by concealing them in milk cans. They could be shipped alongside their milk bearing counterparts, and no one would be the wiser.

One evening my father came home, obviously upset, which was unusual for him. "There's been a robbery," he said, "and all of us who work out of Mound House are suspects." He went on to say that the station was swarming with railroad detectives and investigators and everyone who worked at the station or on the train had been interrogated and investigated. All the employees were suspect whether they worked with passengers or freight. Morale was low and it showed in Dad's demeanor. Our Saturday trips to Carson City ceased because he was so consumed with the investigation. Before the episode of the missing gold, Dad used to tease me, saying, "If you can lift it, (the gold bar), you can have it." It was no longer a joke and anything surrounding the subject was deadly serious.

The investigation became so intense that one of Dad's fellow employees, Mr. Dinan, who used to pick up left-over apples at an orchard in the valley after the harvest, was followed surreptitiously by the detectives. They were sure he had buried the "loot" so they dug up the whole orchard, which, of course, produced nothing.

Eventually, things returned to normal after the investigators could not find a culprit, that is, until one year later. It seems, a former V&T employee, a mailman and baggage handler, attempted to sell a 400 oz. gold bar at a pawnshop in Reno. He was, of course, immediately apprehended, arrested, and subsequently convicted of robbery and a host of other state and federal offenses. The newspapers dubbed him "the dumbest thief on the planet." His arrest had a healing effect on our little community in Mound House, and we all decided that the press had it right.

GRANDMOTHER MAY

My father's mother, Katherine May, was very Irish and very superstitious. If thirteen people showed up at her house for a gathering or party, she would send one home. One could not open an umbrella indoors or rock a rocking chair unless someone was in it. The worse thing that could happen and always caused bad luck was if a bird got into the house. (Years later, when I was in high school, my sister died from pneumonia. Grandmother May always insisted it was because a bird had gotten into the house the day before her death.)

I felt sorry for her because she had broken her leg at an early age and it never healed properly. As a result, she walked with crutches most of her adult life. Dad and his brothers tried to make her life a bit more comfortable by hiring domestics to assist her, but she would immediately dismiss any hired help saying she could take care of herself. To say that she was difficult and cantankerous would be an understatement, but I always liked her and we got along fine. When I was twelve we moved to Reno and I visited her frequently at her home in Sparks, just three miles east.

Grandmother May's best friend was Senator Pat McCarran's mother who was also crippled and walked with crutches. She was paralyzed from the waist down and when she walked with the crutches her lower body would swing from side to side. I don't know how she did it and why she didn't fall but somehow she got around the house. She was also Irish, as ornery as Grandma, and just as superstitious. She also lived alone, for the same reasons my Grandmother did. I don't think either of them could get along with anyone for any length of time. Grandmother May and Mrs. McCarran were best of friends, having many things in common, one of which was bourbon. Whenever I would visit Grandmother May, she'd ask me if I would drive her to see Mrs. McCarran. This meant we had to borrow my uncle Bill's car. If he was working, it was not a problem. We would limit our visit to one hour and return his car and I don't think he ever knew we used it. The car was wonderful, a 1928 Dodge four door, black, square-shaped sedan. It had two flower vases on the inside walls between the front and rear seats, which I thought were classy amenities. What could be nicer than fresh flowers on a Sunday drive?

Mrs. McCarran lived six miles east of Sparks on a ranch in Patrick. Patrick wasn't a town but it had a sign on the highway and railroad to honor Senator Pat McCarran who owned the property. Because I was twelve years old now and a more experienced driver, the trip to the McCarran ranch was not a problem. The only thing I had to worry about was that we had to cross the railroad tracks to get there. My father had instilled the danger of these crossings in my mind, but of course he didn't know I was driving his mother to see her friend. This particular crossing had no warning lights or signals so I would stop the car, look both ways and then dart across the tracks as quickly as possible. When we arrived at the ranch, Mrs. McCarran would greet us and say to me, "Fix your grandmother a wallop," which was code for a water glass filled with bourbon. She would have one also and it always occurred to me that she had had a couple of "wallops" before we arrived. She would walk around the house, her lower body swinging from side to side but never fell down, even after a couple of wallops. They would talk and drink straight whisky from water glasses while I walked around the ranch. We limited the visit to one hour because we had to return Uncle Bill's car before he got home from work. My greatest fear was not that my father would discover that I had driven his mother to the McCarran ranch, but that I had crossed the railroad tracks.

SACRAMENTO BOUND

One day during a visit to Grandmother May's house, she asked me if I could drive her to Sacramento to visit her son Mike. Uncle Mike, like his two brothers, also worked for the Southern Pacific but was domiciled in Sacramento. I didn't realize how far it was from Sparks to Sacramento. I had been to Uncle Mike's many times but we went on a train and it didn't seem to be a long trip, but one-hundred-forty miles on a steep two lane highway through miles of snow sheds became a challenge for a twelve-year-old driver. Thankfully it was summertime, the roads were clear, the traffic sparse, and we made the trip without incident.

After arriving at Uncle Mike's house we realized that we had not told anyone where we were going. My mother thought I was just visiting Grandmother May in Sparks, and I was sure Uncle Bill had missed his car by now. Grandmother decided I should call home and let the family know where we were. When my mother answered the telephone she screamed, "Where are you?" After explaining that we were in Sacramento she said, "Your father wants to talk to you."

I simply told him that Grandmother May wanted to visit Uncle Mike so I drove her to Sacramento in Bill's Dodge. There was a long pause, and then he said firmly, "You stay put and stay out of that car. I'm coming down to get you both. Don't move." He caught the next train to Sacramento and drove us home. It seemed like a longer trip going back to Sparks. Nobody spoke a word all the way. I did get a lecture the next day, but in my father's usual quiet manner, the conversation being more instructive than scolding, and even forgiving. His main concern was for our safety, and of course, he was right.

I know to this day I was his favorite child. I had to be because I tested his tolerance so many times in so many ways, only to have him show patience and understanding. I was the youngest and in his eyes could do no wrong. My father was a wonderful, kind man and I loved him more than anyone in the world.

HOMEBREW

My dad was never a heavy drinker, but he drank, and like many men, during prohibition, made his own beer. I always helped him with the brewing process in the basement of our home in Reno. When one makes beer there are critical times when steps must be taken to insure the final outcome. One of the steps that cannot be delayed is bottling. Unfortunately, my dad's timing was bad and he was called to go on a run for the Southern Pacific at the time the beer was ready. He called me to the basement and patiently explained the procedure: first, you fill the bottles with beer; next, add one teaspoon of sugar to each bottle, then wait for it to settle; insert the bottle into the capper, and pull the handle downward applying the bottle cap. I had watched my father do this in previous batches and felt that I could easily handle the task before me. The only mistake I made was adding one tablespoon of sugar instead of one teaspoon to each bottle.

Two days after I had bottled the beer, my maternal great-grandmother Foster came to visit and planned to stay for a week. This grandmother, unlike Grandmother May, was not only a teetotaler, but was vigorously opposed to anyone drinking alcohol, especially my dad. She had even advised my mother not to marry him because he used alcohol.

We were all in the living room the evening after her arrival when we heard an explosion underneath the house. Grandmother Foster looked up and said, "What was that?"

My mother, knowing very well the origin of the blast, calmly replied, "Oh, that's just the old furnace backfiring. It does it all the time. Don't worry Grandma, it's not a problem." It soon became a problem because the blasts continued one after another until all three cases of beer had blown their tops. It sounded like a war zone in our living room. Then the real problem developed. The odor of beer permeated our home and the "furnace backfiring" excuse was null and void. My grandmother left the living room, proceeded to her bedroom, and packed her suitcase. She departed the next morning obviously disgusted and disappointed with my family, especially my father.

Dad thought the entire incident was funny. His only regret was that he lost three cases of beer. He brewed another batch and showed me the difference between a teaspoon and a tablespoon.

ELMA, THE CARHOP

When I was twelve, I got an after school job as a car hop at the Q Ne Q in Reno. The Q Ne Q was located on Virginia Street, just south of downtown where there's a bend in the road. This establishment was a true drive-in restaurant. There were no tables or counter inside, just a facility where orders were prepared. It was necessary to have a car and drive in, in order to be served.

The trick to being a successful carhop was to be sure the tray would stay put when attached to the auto. I must confess that at first I lost a few orders by not securing the tray correctly, but after a while I got the knack of it and had very few failures.

My favorite customer was Francis Cunningham, the district attorney of Sparks. Mr. Cunningham was a double amputee who had lost his right arm above the wrist and the left above the elbow. In those days there were no sophisticated prostheses as there are nowadays, but he did have hook-like contraptions to take the place of his hands. He always had me wait on him because I made sure his root beer float was in a mug with a handle and that the straw was placed in the drink. In addition, I would hold the mug so that he could get the hook around the handle. This special service must have pleased him. He always left me a five-dollar tip and that was unheard of in 1928. My salary was twenty-five cents per hour.

HAZEN

Hazen, today, is just a wide spot in the road on US Highway 50 located midway between Fernley and Fallon. In the early 1930's it was a railroad town similar to Mound House. Almost everyone who lived there worked for the Southern Pacific except the local merchants and a few people who worked on ranches or in nearby towns.

My family moved to Hazen when I was a freshman in high school. I attended Fallon high school for four years. My father's railroad route at that time was from Hazen to Fallon, however, every two weeks he went to Laws, California near Mammoth.

At first, I thought it was wonderful that I could ride the train every morning from Hazen to Fallon with my Dad and seven of my classmates, however, problems developed primarily because we arrived two hours before classes began. We left Hazen very early in the morning and arrived in Fallon at seven o'clock. School didn't start until nine. Eight freshman students roaming the streets of Fallon was a setup for disaster.

Our first confrontation with the authorities was with school officials. We would go to the gym before school and watch the athletes practice basketball. They would run down the court at high speed and jump to make lay-ups. We thought it would be fun to put a little water on the floor under the basket. When the boys came racing down the court to shoot, they'd hit the water and slide into the mats at the end of the court. We thought it was funny; the coaches did not. We were called into the principal's office, reprimanded, and forbidden anywhere on the school premises until our first class started at nine o'clock.

This meant that we were on the streets of Fallon for two hours with nothing to do. The local stores and shops were not open so we would wander around town and window shop. One day we decided we would pitch pennies to occupy our time before school began. We would stand on the sidewalk at a designated crack and toss a penny three cracks away. The closest penny to the line won all the money. We thought it was harmless fun, however, some of the local Fallon residents did not share our feelings and reported us to the authorities. We were brought to the principal's office again and this time charged with gambling. In addition to pitching pennies, it had also been reported that the "Hazen kids" played cards on the train from Hazen to Fallon, thus the gambling charge. We had developed a bad reputation.

My situation improved when my parents made arrangements for me to live in Fallon during the academic year. I boarded at Minnie Blair's home. Mrs. Blair was the proprietor of the Spudnut shop in Fallon, a popular local hangout. It was a good arrangement for me. I had my own room, a place to study, and didn't have to keep going to the principal's office for disciplinary action. Occasionally, I would have to give up my private room when the Blairs had guests who stayed overnight, but it was a small sacrifice in exchange for the convenience of not making the daily trip from Hazen.

The guest was usually Mitch Armanko, the owner of Armanko's stationery store in Reno. He was a good friend of the Blair family and often came to Fallon to go duck hunting with Mr. Blair. When he came for a visit, I moved out of my room and slept on a cot in the living room. When this happened the first time, I developed a little resentment toward Mr. Armanko, but after I met him, I found him to be one of the nicest men I've ever known. When my parents and I went to Reno Christmas shopping, I went to Armanko's, because in addition to stationery, the store provided a wide variety of gifts. When Mitch Armanko saw me in the store, he approached me and said, "Elma, pick out any item in the store and it will be my Christmas present to you." In view of his generosity, I decided I'd never mention the fact that I had to sleep on a cot whenever he came to Fallon to go duck hunting.

My sister died from pneumonia when I was a senior in high school. She became ill and was subsequently transferred to San Francisco and hospitalized in Saint Francis Hospital. She had the best of care available and had the only oxygen tent in San Francisco at that time.

Antibiotics were not available in 1933 and even with all the efforts of the medical staff she succumbed to the lung infection. After her death I was so devastated I moved back to Hazen to be with my parents.

My mother somehow arranged for a bus to pick up the high school students in Hazen after I moved home. It came at seven o'clock each morning. It was a ninety-minute ride to school because the bus went from Hazen to Lahontan with stops at several ranches to pick up students, and then finally to Fallon. Our bus driver was Bill Bowman, a senior high school student who had a chauffeur's license. Bill was usually accommodating whenever we had an early morning test and didn't want to take it that day. He would find a way to get the bus stuck in the sand and when it didn't appear in Fallon on time, another would be dispatched, but by the time we arrived at school, it was too late the to take the test. Even with all these shenanigans I somehow managed to graduate from Fallon High School in 1933.

FLOYD

I met Floyd when I was a senior in high school. I was living in Hazen, attending high school in Fallon. The Marchmant family, owners the Hazen Hotel, were friends of the Smalley family in Reno. The Marchmants had three children, two daughters and a son, the girls being friends of mine, and the son a friend of Floyd. At that time he was attending the University of Nevada. One weekend he drove to Hazen to visit the Marchmant family and that is when I was introduced to Floyd Smalley.

My first impression was that of any young girl meeting a six-foot-three-inch, handsome college man with dark curly hair and an engaging manner. I was smitten. The weekend ended and we returned to our respective residences. We didn't meet again until I enrolled as a freshman in the University of Nevada. He was a member of Sigma Chi Sigma fraternity at the university and asked me to one of the fraternity dances. Following that, we started dating on a regular basis.

I was enrolled in a five-year program that included three years at the University of Nevada and two at Stanford. This was a medical program that led to a nursing degree with a Bachelor of Science. Unfortunately, I became ill during my third year and had to drop out of school for six months. I had appendicitis but the condition was not diagnosed until my appendix ruptured, resulting in peritonitis. Antibiotics were not available; the treatment was surgery. The doctors inserted a rubber tube into the infected area, allowing drainage through an incision in my lower abdomen. The contraption stuck out of my belly about two inches. The protruding tube was covered with a three-inch dressing of cotton and gauze that absorbed the yellowish-brown foul smelling drainage. Every two or three days I went to the doctor's office for a dressing change. He would grasp the rubber tube with forceps, pull it out about a half-inch, and cut off the same length that he had advanced. This procedure went on for three months. During one of these office visits, I asked the doctor, "How long was that tube you put in me?"

He just smiled and said, "Be patient. We put in a long piece, and it'll all come out in time. You're dong fine." As time went on the drainage decreased and the visits became less frequent. One day when he pulled the tube to advance it, the last half-inch popped out. He remarked, "Good, it's done its job and we're finished with that tube." After that, the drainage continued to diminish and I was able to dress it myself at home. Finally it stopped completely and for the first time in five months, I no longer had to wear a bandage on my lower abdomen.

A VISIT TO MY AUNT

Following my episode of appendicitis and long con-valescence, I became depressed. I had to drop out of the university, couldn't work or do much of anything because of the rubber drain in my lower abdomen. My mother was worried about my mental health, so after the drain was finally removed and I was more mobile, she suggested we visit her sister in Templeton, a small town in central California near San Luis Obispo. A change of scenery seemed appealing so I agreed to make the trip. We took the train from Reno to Oakland, transferred to a San Francisco bound ferry, and took a bus to the Southern Pacific depot at Third and Townsend, where we boarded the train to central California. The trip up to this point was uneventful; however, after we left San

Jose an accident occurred. A truck crossing the railroad tracks was hit by our train at an intersection in a rural area where many secondary roads crossed the tracks. The engine and first two cars were derailed. The cars broke loose from the engine and flipped over on their sides, but the locomotive continued upright plowing forward through the underbrush and finally stopped perched on Highway 101. (I later read an article in Reader's Digest which was written by a gentleman who was driving on Highway 101 at the time of the accident. He described an incredible sight–a locomotive parked in the middle of a major California highway.)

Our car was still on the tracks and continued to roll forward after we felt the impact of the collision. After the train stopped, I looked out the window and saw a man lying along the tracks with a wide gash in his abdomen. He was disemboweled in the accident and there was a large amount of blood around him. It was a horrible sight and I knew he was dead. Amazingly, there was nobody near him. He was all alone just lying there with his intestines exposed. I got up from my seat, left the train and walked toward him. It was a pitiful sight and

I felt embarrassed seeing a helpless person in that condition. I took off my coat and covered him. I don't know why. I just thought it was the right thing to do.

Mother and I got off the train and we walked the few yards to the highway. By this time many cars had stopped and people were standing gawking at the accident. Two men approached us and inquired if we were passengers on the train and asked if we knew what had happened. They were investigators for aviation accidents and were driving to Los Angeles to evaluate an airplane crash. After talking to my mother for a few minutes, they offered to drive us to Templeton which was on their way to Los Angeles. My mother gratefully accepted their offer, but told them we had to inform the conductor on the train that we were not injured and had made arrangements for other transportation to our destination. In the confusion it was difficult to find the conductor, but she eventually located him and we were cleared to leave. Our two good Samaritans were eager to be on their way to Los Angeles. They were apparently on a tight schedule and delay was going to cause them a late arrival. I have never traveled that fast in an automobile. They must have been driving ninety miles an hour. My mother, who was terrified, told me she wished she had waited for another train.

Even with the delay caused by the accident, we arrived in Templeton at about the time the train was scheduled to arrive, thanks to our high-speed highway driver. We were surprised to learn that the officials and railroad personnel had not been informed of the train accident. My aunt was waiting for us at the train depot in Templeton and was surprised when we arrived by automobile rather than rail. After hearing the details of the accident she was relieved we had arrived safely. Our visit with my aunt was delightful and therapeutic even after experiencing a train wreck and losing my coat along the way.

MY WEDDING

Floyd and I were in a dilemma. We wanted to get married, however, I wanted to complete my senior year at the university and Floyd had taken a job teaching seventh and eighth grades in Austin. The problem was my father. He had no objections to the marriage, but he was adamant that if we got married we should not live apart. We suggested that I could live at home and complete my senior year and Floyd could continue teaching in Austin, and we could see each other on weekends. My father would not hear of it. People who got married should live together, period! He was firm in his belief and there was no compromise or negotiation.

We then formulated "plan B." We would elope and not tell my father. The plan was for Floyd and me, along with Rita and Rocter Fuhrman, designated bridesmaid and best man, to drive to Carson City on a Saturday morning in August and "tie the knot." The Fuhrmans were our best friends and supportive of our clandestine venture. It was rumored that the Ormsby County Clerk, Mrs. Legget, had a reputation of never taking a day off and was always available to issue marriage licenses. She took applications and required forms home with her after office hours and issued the licenses from there evenings and weekends. We were told that upon request, Mrs. Legget would see to it that notification would not appear in the vital statistics section of the newspaper. She had developed a system to remove a particular license from the stack of marriage licenses and insert it into a pile of other county documents in which the press was not interested. "Plan B" definitely called for this procedure. We also understood that she never refused a gratuity for her extra effort and cooperation.

We drove directly to her home, knowing the County Clerk's office would be closed for the weekend. Arriving at her house, we eagerly knocked on the door, but there was no answer. We inquired at a neighbor's house and were told she went to Reno for the first time in twenty years. The neighbor said, "If you want a marriage license just wait on the front porch. She'll be back soon." So, we parked the car in front of her house and the four of us sat on her front porch for four hours until she returned from Reno.

As she walked up the steps she said, "I suppose you want a marriage license."

All four of us stood up and in unison answered, "Yes." We filled out the application, paid the license fee plus the obligatory tip, and thanked her before the fact for bypassing the press.

We obviously didn't want a big wedding, but because I was a practicing Catholic it was imperative that we be married in the Church. Floyd had been baptized as an infant and even though he had never practiced the faith, professing our vows before a priest was not a problem. Rocter and Rita were not Catholic. With our marriage license in hand, we drove to St. Theresa's Church downtown Carson City. The four of us walked to the rectory and knocked on the door. The door opened and standing before us was Monsignor Wientjes, a priest I had never met. We introduced ourselves and he asked what he could do for us, and I replied, "We would like to get married."

"Oh, I see. Well, perhaps you should come in and we'll talk about that." We were seated and he proceeded to lecture us for more than an hour about responsibility, commitment, raising our children Catholic, and a host of other doctrines. He was particularly focused on Floyd, encouraging him to be confirmed, start attending Mass, and becoming active in the church, emphasizing the importance of a family united with Christ as a foundation for marriage. Rita and Rocter just sat patiently and nodded whenever Father posed a rhetorical question.

My greatest concern was that he was going to ask for our address in Reno or mention our names to a priest there, which might lead to my father's discovering we had gotten married. Fortunately, he didn't ask for any identification other than our names, which were on the marriage license anyway. Suddenly, he said, "Okay, stand up." He read the ritual words from his prayer book, we exchanged vows and within two minutes on August 15, 1937, I became Mrs. Floyd Smalley, the best decision I ever made in my life.

MY "SECOND" MARRIAGE

After our marriage in Carson City, we lived a rather covert life. I went back to school at the University of Nevada, and Floyd continued teaching in Austin. Our friends, the Fuhrmans, lived in Reno and had a second home at Lake Tahoe. Whenever they went to the lake for weekends, they would give us a key to their house in Reno. Floyd would drive in from Austin and we would spend weekends together. This arrangement went on for nearly a year, however, after four months I told my mother the story of our wedding. She was understanding and didn't tell my father. My greatest fear was that I would get pregnant, but we were lucky and managed to keep our secret concealed.

At the end of my senior year, we decided it was time to get honest and somehow let my dad know we were married without actually revealing that the nuptials had already taken place. After some serious plotting we came up with a scheme. Above all, we insisted we did not want a big wedding with a lot of fanfare. We'd prefer a private ceremony at Lake Tahoe with just a best man and bridesmaid in attendance. Mom pretended she was disappointed but succeeded in convincing Dad that if that is what we wanted, so be it. Having jumped that hurdle, we drove to the lake, had lunch, and spent the day sightseeing. Upon returning to Reno, I told my father we were now man and wife and I would be moving to Austin to live with Floyd. He hugged me and said, "Fine, Elma. That's the way it should be." So my second wedding was really not a wedding at all. It was just a ruse to disclose the first wedding that had occurred nearly a year previously. Somehow we managed to pull off the charade and as far as I know, Dad never discovered our little secret.

AUSTIN

After our "second marriage," with the blessings of my father, I moved to Austin to live with Floyd. Before I left Reno, my father gave me a lecture about small town folks and their attitudes toward teachers. The main thrust of the conversation was that the mentality of such towns dictated that teachers and their wives be pillars of the community and not use alcohol. In other words he was telling me to behave and never be seen doing anything that would jeopardize our position in the community. I thanked him, packed my bags, and set out to join my husband.

Upon arriving in Austin, I learned that the community was giving us a reception to welcome Floyd and his new bride. I wished my father could have attended.

Compared to these folks, we were amateur drinkers. Mr. Hiskey, owner of the Hiskey Stage Lines and president of the school board, hosted the reception. He had the largest and nicest home in Austin which was impressively decorated and furnished for this little mining town. But all evening, I kept thinking of my father who was concerned that schoolteachers shouldn't drink. Every alcoholic potable available in the state was served, and most of the guests imbibed without reservation.

Floyd had been in Austin two years living with the principal and his wife until I arrived. We rented a motel where we lived as honeymooners, although technically we were not newlyweds. We knew the motel was temporary housing because it was the end of the school year and Floyd had accepted a position in Wells for the following September. I lived in Austin for only two weeks, but I loved it. It was an old mining town built on the side of a mountain very close to the mines. There were a few nice houses but most of the buildings were wooden shacks.

Main Street could have been the set for a classic Western movie. Most of the businesses were along this street, which, with its wooden sidewalks and bustling Austin Hotel, doubled as US Highway 50. There were seven churches in town but they were far outnumbered by the saloons.

I have a friend, Eldora Lewis, who visited me while I was in Austin. We have been friends since the fourth grade and got together every year thereafter. I think she was somewhat shocked when she saw the town. Our motel did not have indoor plumbing nor did most of the homes in town at that time. Our toilet, an outhouse, was located about thirty yards behind the motel. The distance was not the problem; the issue was the group of Indians that congregated behind the motel everyday to consume alcohol. Although the parties were entertaining and fun to watch, which we did from the window of our room, we were a little afraid to walk through the imbibing group to use the facilities. The problem, however, was solved when the owner of the motel was arrested for selling alcohol to the Indians, which was illegal at that time.

We moved back to Reno for the summer. I didn't mention to my father that at the reception in Austin the school board gave us a cocktail shaker and six glasses for a wedding present. I just told him the town folks were very congenial.

After the summer session was over at the university, we packed the car again and drove to Wells in search of a place to live.

Elma's parents,
James Alvin May and Amy Eliza Harding

Mound House
Nevada, 1920's.
Courtesy of the
Nevada Historical
Society

The Turntable in Mound House. Courtesy of the Nevada Historical Society

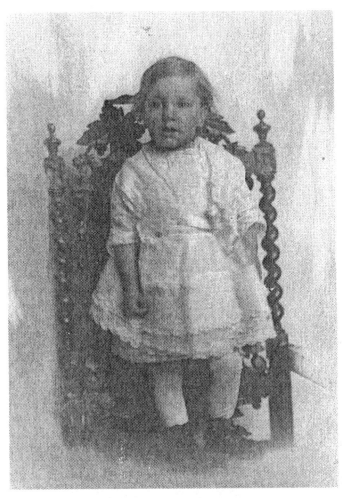

Elma's parents had this picture taken because she had pneumonia and they thought she would not survivel.

The tram from the gypsum mine to the mill in Mound House. Courtesy of the Nevada Historical Society

Elma's First Communion

Locomotive #2156 in Mound House. Courtesy of the Nevada Historical Society.

The gypsum Mill in Mound House. Courtesy of the Nevada Historic Society.

Mound House Railroad Station, now located at the Carson City Railroad Museum.
Courtesy of the Nevada Historical Society.

Hazen, Nevada, early 1900's
Courtesy of the Nevada Historical Society.

Saint Theresa's Catholic Church in Carson City,
where Elma and Floyd were married in 1937.
Courtesy of the Nevada Historic Society

Elma with her children, Jim and Linda.

Elma and Floyd

The Smalley's
fortieth wedding
anniversary

Elma at home in Reno, 2005

WELLS

Wells is located in eastern Nevada, seventy-five miles west of the Utah border. The surrounding landscape looks similar to most of Nevada, sagebrush covered valleys and pinion covered mountains. Driving from west to east one traverses a series of large valleys and mountain ranges. The entire state is in the Great Basin, which means that all the rainfall and melted snow never drains into the Atlantic or Pacific. It ends up in lakes, most of which dry up during the summer months. Winters are more severe in eastern Nevada, and windier, with more snow than the rest of the state.

We rented an apartment in Wells. It was in a four-unit complex. The principal and his wife lived in one unit, a teacher and his wife lived in the second, a highway worker and his wife lived in the third apartment, and we occupied the fourth. It was comfortable, a step up from the motel in Austin and no Indians in the backyard. It was good to have other teachers in the building with whom we became good friends and shared common interests. Floyd and the principal used to listen to football games on the radio on Saturdays, but a problem arose because the highway worker and his wife cleaned their apartment while the game was on. They would vacuum for what seems like hours, interrupting the radio reception in the other apartments. The vacuum cleaner, provided by the landlord, was kept in a utility closet on the lower floor and was to be used by all the tenants. After a few Saturdays, Floyd and the principal solved the problem of electronic interference. They would sneak down to the closet, confiscate the vacuum cleaner, and keep it in our apartment until the football game was over.

The only other problem renting the apartment was that we went to Reno for three months when school was out. The landlord agreed to hold our unit through the summer months, but we had to remove all our belongings so he could rent it on a daily basis while we were away. When school was out in June, we had to pack up all our belongings and store them until fall. The condition of the apartment was less than pristine when we returned, but we would get it cleaned up and move back in. We lived in Wells for three years and repeated this procedure every summer so we could attend summer sessions at the U of N.

NORTH FORK

When I moved to Wells, I had to accept substitute teaching jobs because I was married, and in 1938 married women could not be hired in permanent teaching positions. The Nevada school system's policy stated that only men and single women were eligible to become permanent teachers. It was felt that a man was the head of the family and had to support his wife and children, and single women had to support themselves. Married women were supposed to be housewives and homemakers. I guess that mandate was the reason women were branded, "Old Maid School Teachers."

I was occasionally called to substitute for a day or two if one of the teachers was ill or had a valid excuse not to teach that particular day. One day in February I received a call asking if I would be interested in a long-term position in North Fork, in the Island Mountain School District. The district was north of Elko, close to the Idaho border in northeastern Nevada. It was a one-room schoolhouse, accommodating grades one through eight. Even though I was apprehensive thinking about teaching eight grades in one room, my main concern was where I was going to live. I was living in Wells, which is more than 100 miles southeast of North Fork, and driving such a distance daily was not an option. The winters in northern Nevada were severe and the roads to North Fork were closed for days after a snowstorm. Fortunately, the superintendent of the Island Mountain School District understood my situation and arranged for me to live on the R.Y. Reed Ranch, two miles from the school. Floyd and I discussed the job offer and we decided that it was an opportunity for me to have a real position so I accepted the offer. I would live on the ranch and commute to Wells on weekends.

I don't recall the exact salary, but I do remember it was less than one-hundred dollars per month. There was an additional perk, however. The Reed family was compensated for my room and board by the school district.

The North Fork school was located two miles west of Highway 225 north of Elko. The ranch, my newly designated residence, was another two miles beyond the school. My class consisted of five students from two adjacent ranches, the Vega's and the Reed's: two girls from the Reed ranch, grades five and eight; two boys, third and fourth graders, and a eight grade girl from the Vega ranch.

Prior to my arrival, there had been a dispute between the Vegas and Reeds concerning the location of the school. The Vegas insisted the school was closer to the Reed ranch, so after some negotiation, the school was moved off the secondary dirt road that led to the Reed ranch a quarter-mile closer to the Vega ranch. As a result, there was no road to the school. It was now located on a mound in the middle of a sagebrush flat. The ranchers felt no need for a road since all the children rode horses to school.

I drove our 1934 Chevrolet from Wells to the Reed ranch in February 1938. At first sight that northern

Nevada landscape appeared bleak; but as I let the view penetrate my senses, I saw oceans of silver-gray sagebrush against blue hills highlighting the magnificence of the desert, and snow-capped mountain peaks glistening in the sunshine. It was quiet and calming. I had lived in Nevada all my life, but for the first time I realized this desert was a vast and glorious expanse of color and beauty. I didn't realize it then but I was to live in a fascinating place.

Two miles after I turned off the main highway and headed west, I saw the North Fork school for the first time, sitting in the middle of a vast sagebrush valley. I had a flashing thought, "Oh God, what have I gotten into?" Fortunately, the road was open and despite a little snow and a few potholes and ruts, I arrived safely at the Reed ranch.

I drove to the main house and as I got out of the car, Mrs. Reed walked toward me, arms extended, embracing me, saying, "You're welcome here. Thank you for coming to teach our children." She was a large buxom woman, her graying hair pulled back into a bun. Her piercing blue eyes made direct contact with me making me feel she was totally engaged when we spoke. "Come with me, I'll show you to your room."

We entered the house and as we stepped into the living room, the Reed girls were waiting for introductions. They too, embraced me, and said, "Thank you for coming Mrs. Smalley."

Mary, the eighth grader, said to me, "I'm so happy you came. I want to go to high school and without a teacher I would not be able to finish the eighth grade."

Mrs. Reed then took me upstairs to my room. The first thing I saw when she opened the door was a beautiful patchwork quilt on the bed. I gasped with joy, and complimented and thanked her for providing me such a magnificent piece of handiwork. She lowered her head and said humbly, "I'm glad you like it Elma. It was my mother's."

One of the first orders of business was to figure out how I was going to get from the ranch to school each morning. There was only one solution. I had to ride a horse, which posed a major problem. I had never ridden a horse and knew nothing about horses or horseback riding. The oldest Reed girl showed me how to saddle the horse and gave me an elementary riding lesson. My biggest challenge was getting the cinch tight enough to keep the saddle in place.

There were four fences between the ranch and the school. That meant there were four gates that had to be opened and closed on my morning journey. I had to dismount at each gate and every time I did the saddle would slide sideways and fall to the side; I'd have to re-adjust it at every stop. I was afraid it would hurt the horse if I pulled too tight, but I soon learned the old mare was distending her belly purposely, only to return it to its original girth once I mounted.

The first day of school was predicable. I introduced myself, welcomed the five students, and outlined the basic rules of behavior I expected them to follow. I then sat down at my desk, open the drawer, and saw the snake. At first I thought it was fake or dead, but when it moved I realized this was my rite of passage. I grabbed the snake behind the head, held it up to the students and asked, "Does this belong to anyone here?" Five children looked at me with wide-open eyes, but no response. After a slight pause, I asked the two Vega boys to come forward, take the snake outside, and release it. I was tested and I think I won. I never had another prank from the students, however, I still had some surprises awaiting me back at the ranch.

When Mrs. Reed's husband had died two years previously during a snowstorm, no one could get in or out of the ranch. She had him placed in a wooden box in one of the outbuildings for nearly two weeks before he could be transported to Elko for burial. She alone assumed the duties of ranch manager after his death.

She had seven hired men who tended the cattle and sheep on the ranch. They did all the physical work: mending fences, rounding up strays, and building corrals and loading ramps for cattle. They all lived together in the bunkhouse. From the first day I met the cowboys, it was apparent that some of them were pranksters and I soon learned that my first impression was correct. One day after school, a cowboy named Hank, approached me and said, "Elma, would you like to see how branding is done?" Hank was a tall thin man, six feet plus, with a dark tanned face and sun wrinkled cheeks.

I wanted to be friendly, so I said, "Sure Hank, I'd love to watch," totally unaware of what branding entailed.

The men built a huge charcoal fire and placed branding irons in the hot coals, heating them until they were bright red. The initials RYR were on the bottom of each iron. The calves were led toward the fire one by one, wrestled to the ground, and had their legs tied so they would be lying flat. Two men would hold the calf down while a third man would pull a rod from the fire and plunge the hot poker onto the calf's thigh. Of course, the immobile creature would squeal in pain and jerk as if it were having a seizure. A cloud of smoke from burned hair and singed flesh would permeate the air and the odor was nauseating. Each time the cowboy pushed the branding iron onto the calf's thigh all eyes were on me, awaiting my reaction. It took all the emotional control I had to stay calm and refrain from retching. They had their fun that day with a greenhorn, ranch style.

The cowboys were also a problem for Mrs. Reed. When they went into Elko on the weekends, they would return to the ranch drunk. One night they arrived at the ranch and one of the boys was so drunk he had passed out. Two others carried him toward the main house and laid him in the front yard. I observed this from my bedroom window and decided to join the party surrounding the unconscious cowboy. I suggested, "Why don't we put candles around him so when he wakes up, he'll think it's a wake." The ranch had an adequate supply of candles to provide light during the frequent power failures, so we placed candles all around him. They had nearly burned out by the time he awakened. What he saw startled him. He jumped up confused, and staggered to the bunkhouse. I don't think he ever forgave us, but at least we all had a hearty laugh.

After I mastered the saddle straps, and got down to the business of teaching, the daily ride to school became a pleasant way to start the day. It was cold but the desert always offered something new. The morning sunrises were a glorious mix of yellow and orange; coyotes, rabbits, deer, ground squirrels and a variety of birds were common sightings along the way. As I passed the cows, I always looked at the RYR scar on their thighs and remembered the day I was initiated to ranch life.

I got to school early each day to start a fire in the wood stove and prepare the day's lessons. The two Reed girls also rode horses to school, but they came later after they did their morning chores. One of their duties was to feed the "bummer lambs." These babies had either lost their mothers or were abandoned and had to be bottle fed to survive until they could eat by themselves.

The decision to move the North Fork school off the secondary road created an additional problem for me. My plan was, weather permitting, to return to Wells to see my husband on weekends. I had driven to the Reed ranch where I parked my car. After I learned that I could not drive to school because of weather conditions and the absence of a road, I formulated plan "B." I would, with the help of my sturdy Chevy, forge a new road. I rode horseback Monday through Thursday, but on Friday if it wasn't snowing, I drove the Chevy. I'd turn off the gravel road and plow through the sagebrush, bouncing along toward the schoolhouse. At first, the brush would scrape the oil pan on the bottom of the car, but with continued use, the new road got better and better, week after week. By the time my assignment was completed in June, I had created a passable trail to the school for my faithful auto to ride upon.

The cowboy pranksters designed another unique ploy to intimidate me. They knew I left the ranch every Friday after school to go to Wells to be with Floyd on the weekend, returning Sunday evening. Two of the gates I had to open to get in and out of the ranch were close together, creating a narrow strip of pasture, approximately fifty feet wide. I would drive to the first gate, stop the car, open the gate and drive through, close it, and walk to the second gate, open it, return to my car and proceed through the second gate. One Sunday when I returned to the ranch from Wells, I pulled up at the gate and noticed a bull in the narrow pasture between the two gates. I had never seen the bull in this pasture, in fact there were never any cattle in this narrow strip of land. Then, I glanced to the right and saw the cowboys sitting on the hillside looking down at the gates, the bull, and yours truly, and knew immediately I had been set up. The pranksters had moved the bull into the narrow pasture to make my passage between the gates a challenge. I sat in my car for a few minutes to contemplate my next move.

I looked at the bull, got out of the car, opened the first gate, and drove through. I got out of the car again, closed the first gate, drove a few feet to the second gate and looked at the bull again. He was about thirty yards away, grazing and looking benign enough. I opened the door gingerly and wedged a box of Kleenex into the hinges to hold it open. I ran to the second gate, opened it and scurried back to my car. I jumped in and slammed the door. I drove through, closed the gate, and when I looked up I saw the boys on the hill. I thought to myself, "boys will be boys," and living in this isolation what else did they have to do on Sunday evenings. I looked at the bull and he hadn't moved and was still grazing. He had never been in this pasture and was taking advantage of the virgin grass. I waved to the cowboys and drove on to the ranch.

The Nevada School Board policy in 1938 stated that every eighth grade student had to be tested and evaluated by a deputy superintendent before entering high school. There were two eighth grade students in my class, Mary Reed and Elizabeth Vega. One evening I received a phone call from Floyd informing me that the deputy superintendent, a friend of his, was scheduled to make a surprise visit to my school the following day for the eighth graders' high school evaluation. I decided I had to make an impression on this esteemed official, so the next morning I dressed in my usual riding garb, but in addition, I rolled up my best dress and put it into the saddlebag. Upon arriving at school, I changed clothes and for the first day ever at North Fork, I taught school dressed like a lady. I greeted the deputy superintendent upon his arrival. He did his evaluation and must have been impressed because both girls were admitted to high school. I don't know if the dress helped, but after all these years, I still choose to believe it contributed to the favorable evaluation.

One Friday, I drove my Chevy to school, planning to drive to Wells after school to spend the weekend with Floyd. I stayed late to clean up and complete some routine paperwork. All the children had saddled their horses and left for home. When I finished my work, I locked the school and got into the car. I pushed the starter and nothing happened. Panic time! I was alone in the middle of the desert with no horse, no telephone, and a dead car. My first thought was to walk back to the ranch, but

I wanted desperately to visit Floyd in Wells. Hopelessly, I lifted the hood. I saw the problem immediately. The battery cable was broken; my road-building project had taken its toll. Bouncing through the sagebrush had twisted and worn the cable until it snapped. Perhaps I could improvise. With two pairs of pliers, I borrowed a piece of barbed wire from the horse corral behind the school. I wrapped it around the battery terminal and secured the other end to the frame of the car. I prayed, pushed the starter and the Chevy started on the first try. I drove as though I were walking on eggs from the school through the sagebrush, and by the time I reached the secondary road I had gained a smidgen of confidence. When I finally reached the highway to Elko, I relaxed, increased speed, and headed towards Wells. I felt smug, creative, ingenious, and self-sufficient. Floyd was incredulous. With a sigh of relief he obtained a new battery cable and repaired my car.

One day in early summer, I returned to the ranch on horseback and heard laughter and frolicking in the barn. The cowboys had sheared the sheep. The wool was put in large bulky burlap bags. The men would jump down from the second story of the barn and land on the bags of wool, tamping it down. The children ran around hopping and jumping on the bags to compress the wool. Of course I joined in and helped with the wool stomp. What great fun it was! However, returning to the house, I discovered I was covered with ticks. Mrs. Reed came to my rescue and patiently touched a hot match to each tick saying, "Good, he backed out." She removed fifteen ticks in all.

The Vega children were excellent students. They were polite, cooperative, but naïve beyond belief. They had never been to Elko, which was a mere fifty miles south of North Fork; in fact, they had never been off the Vega ranch. Their only contacts in the entire world were parents, the Reed girls, each other, and yours truly. When teaching government, I frequently mentioned "Uncle Sam," thinking that everyone knew I was referring to our federal government. I soon learned one of the Vega students thought Uncle Sam was my uncle. I realized then that when children are so isolated from the world and have limited contacts, nothing can be taken for granted.

I visited the Vega ranch one time. I was surprised when I walked into the kitchen and saw chickens running around eating off the floor. The Vegas were old country people, hard working, honest, and generous. They lived as their parents had lived in the Pyrenees between Spain and France. They were sheepherders and ranchers and lived life in the Basque tradition.

When I think about my first teaching assignment, I realize I learned more than any of my students. I was initiated to ranch life by two wonderful families, teased by mischievous cowboys, learned to ride a horse, and built a road. Except for the ticks, it was a great experience.

A LUNCH WITH UNCLE

The semester had ended in Wells the last week in May so Floyd went to Reno and stayed at his parents' home where I would join him as soon as my assignment was finished in mid-June. I decided to stay at the ranch for the remaining two weeks of my teaching job. In order to be with Floyd on the weekends I'd have to drive all the way to Reno, and besides we wouldn't be able to spend much time together because he had taken a job at the local brickyard.

I must have been moping around looking forlorn the first weekend I spent on the ranch, so much so, the Reed girls approached me and asked if I'd like to take a trail ride the following weekend. I jumped at the opportunity and asked where we were going.

The older girl, Mary, said, "Just over the hill to Tuscarora to have lunch at our uncle's ranch. It's another Reed ranch that belongs to our dad's brother." I agreed and at 6:00 A.M. Saturday morning we saddled our horses, filled our canteens, strapped on our chaps, and set out through the desert. The "just over the hill" turned out to be about fifteen miles over a mountain, and through a canyon of sagebrush, pinion pine and junipers. We arrived about eleven o'clock, met the family, had lunch, and took a short rest.

Considering the distance we had to cover to return home before dark, we didn't tarry long. We extended our thanks for their hospitality, bade our hosts farewell and mounted our horses for the long ride back.

By this time, the sun was high, beating on us mercilessly, as we headed over the hills. We had ridden for about an hour when I detected some friction developing between the girls. The younger said, "I told you we should have taken the other trail."

"Is everything all right?" I asked.

Mary replied, "I think we're in the wrong canyon."

I was panic-stricken. Here we were miles from civilization, stranded in the Nevada desert, with nothing to eat and the water in our canteens dangerously low. I had visions of Floyd combing the desert for his loving wife and finding only a sun-bleached skeleton that had been stripped clean by vultures. I swallowed the lump in my throat and whispered, "What are we going to do?"

The older girl, Mary, answered, " Well, we may be lost, but the horses aren't. We'll give them their heads and they'll take us home."

I had my doubts as I removed the bridle, got a death grip on the saddle horn, and turned my life over to three "dumb animals."

The route the horses chose was not a forged trail. Some of the terrain was so steep that they would straighten their front legs and slide down the rocky slopes. I held on to the saddle horn with all my might, leaned back, and prayed. As we made our way through thorny chaparral and under low hanging tree limbs, I was nearly knocked out of the saddle a number of times. The time passed slowly and as the terrain smoothed out a bit I must have dozed off for a few minutes. Then the horses picked up their pace, first accelerating to a trot, then a gentle gallop. When I opened my eyes, I couldn't believe what I saw. The Reed ranch was directly ahead. The beasts knew exactly where they were and carried us right to the corral. They were home, and thank the Good Lord, so were we.

I dismounted carefully to protect my blistered hands and saddle sore behind. I gave my mare a big hug and said gratefully, "Thanks so much. You're not such a dumb animal after all." I also realized that this naïve teacher had learned a valuable lesson that day from her savvy students.

When we walked in the house at six o'clock, Mrs. Reed inquired, "How was your trip?"

"Great," I replied, "and the lunch was delicious." Nothing was said about our misadventure, and thank heavens, she didn't notice the horses had no bridles.

HAWTHORNE

Floyd's goal as an educator was to be an administrator, but he realized he needed a few years of classroom experience before he could advance to such a position. An opportunity presented itself during our third year in Wells. The principal of the Hawthorne grammar school resigned and Floyd, after evaluating the situation, felt it was a chance for advancement and applied for the position.

I had never been to Hawthorne. All I knew was what I had heard from friends. It was a small town with a naval ammunition depot located near Walker Lake. My first impression of the town was not a good one. Floyd and I attended the school board meeting where the members were to decide who would get the job as principal. There were several applicants. The school board voted behind closed doors, and when they returned to the boardroom, it was announced that Floyd Smalley had been awarded the position. After the announcement, one of the board members, a woman, walked up to me, looked me directly in the eyes and said, "I want you to know that I did not vote for your husband." I really didn't know what to say, so I didn't say anything. Floyd explained to me later that the former principal had resigned, primarily because of tension, quarreling, and disagreement on the school board. This same woman, who apparently couldn't get along with anyone, had caused most of the problems. Because Floyd and the former principal were good friends, the outspoken board member apparently thought we had been forewarned about her problems with the board and was just being defensive. At the time, Floyd was aware of her idiosyncrasies, but I didn't know anything about her, the school board, or its problems, so I nicknamed her, "The Queen of Hawthorne." I honestly believe she thought she had real power and authority because she was a member of the school board in Hawthorne, Nevada. She mellowed throughout the years and we actually became much closer, although we were never real friends. I have often wondered if she regretted making that remark to me on my first day in Hawthorne, especially years later when Floyd became the Mineral County Superintendent of Schools.

After this rough start, Hawthorne turned out to be a wonderful place for our family. We saw many changes in the community during the twenty-eight years we lived there. When we arrived in 1941 there was one grammar school with 60 students and four teachers. When we left there were five grammar schools, 3000 students, and over 100 teachers. The main reason for the increases, of course, was the expansion of the naval base. We arrived in August 1941; in December, World War II began and Hawthorne became a naval ammunition supply center for the entire west coast fleet in the Pacific. The desert surrounding the town became speckled with sand mounds containing underground bunkers in which ammunition was stored. The government instituted a massive building program to provide housing for the influx of civilian workers and the naval base expanded to accommodate the increase in navy and marine personnel and their families. The government constructed rows of attractive single-family homes and the base resembled a subdivision, much like its contemporary counterparts. Paved streets, utilities, rows of trees, attractive landscaping, lawns, parks and playgrounds were all provided for the families of civilian and military personnel. The government even constructed a grammar school on the base so children would not have to be transported to a school in town. Even though the government owned the building, the Hawthorne school district operated the school, providing teachers and administration. In addition, they built an attractive row of larger brick homes which we called "officers' row." A navy captain who was in charge of the base had the biggest home, a three-story house at the head of officers' row. There were smaller homes for the junior officers.

The marines provided security for the base. They were formal and professional as they performed their duties, checking everyone who entered and exited the base. They looked trim and handsome in their tailored uniforms. The officers received a formal salute when they passed through the gate and they returned the military formality in an equally snappy manner.

Security on the base and surrounding area of Hawthorne was a serious matter. There was always the possibility of sabotage. The handling and transporting of ammunition was a dangerous chore and taken very seriously by the military and security personnel. During the war there were several explosions in the storage bunkers and some of the workers were killed and others injured. I would occasionally substitute teach on the base. Floyd and I had security clearances and were issued passes to enter the compound. One morning I drove to the gate and presented my pass to the marine. He looked at it, backed away from my car and said politely, "Sorry Ma'am, this pass is outdated and expired and I cannot allow you to enter the base."

I replied, "You've got to let me come in. I'm a school teacher and the children will be waiting for me."

He repeated, "Your pass has expired and I cannot permit you to enter this secure area." I stared back and said, "Call the captain."

"Yes Ma'am." He turned, entered the guard booth, and picked up the telephone. When he came out, he told me to pull my car to the side of the road so others could pass and informed me that he had spoken with the captain who would arrive shortly. A few moments later the captain did appear in a jeep. He resolved the problem, but I noticed that even the captain had to sign papers to permit me to enter. I had to get an updated pass that day before I could leave the base. The navy ran a very tight ship.

I didn't take a full time teaching position until after our children were in school. I was a stay-at-home Mom and I loved it. We rented a house the first year we were there–the first real house we had lived in since our marriage. We had lived with our parents in Reno, in a motel in Austin, in an apartment in Wells, and I had boarded on a cattle ranch in North Fork. What a luxury it was to have a house that we called home.

After one year, we knew we were going to stay in Hawthorne, and so we decided to build our own house. Floyd found a catalog that featured pre-cut homes from a company in Portland, Oregon. We picked out the one we wanted and had it shipped by rail to Hawthorne. The model we selected had two bedrooms, one bath, a living room, dining area, and a washroom. Our future home arrived in one boxcar at Thorn, the railroad terminal for Hawthorne where the ammunition was shipped in and out of the supply depot. The Southern Pacific put the boxcar containing our home on a siding so we could unload the pieces of pre-cut lumber and accessories. We had a trailer that we pulled with our car. Driving down the siding between two sets of railroad tracks to the boxcar was no problem. We loaded the first load into the trailer and then realized we could not turn around because we were in between two sets of tracks. We had to back out between the tracks for almost a quarter mile. Backing a trailer requires skill and experience and we had neither. We discovered that a trailer turns the opposite direction of the car's steering wheel. Eventually we figured it out and Floyd improved as time went on. We made many trips up and down between those tracks, but finally, all the items were at our home site. It was a huge mound of assorted material, a big jigsaw puzzle, and now all we had to do was put it together.

We set out to do just that: put it together. With the directions in one hand and a hammer in the other, we spent an entire summer building our new home. Floyd was the carpenter and I was his assistant. We had a little help from coach Wilber Troy, a teacher friend of Floyd, but essentially we did most of the work. Because gypsum wallboard was not available in those days, lath and plaster was used for the interior walls. I was the lath lady. I nailed thin strips of wood horizontally on the two-by-four walls in all the rooms. Plastering required a professional and we realized we would have to get help with this phase of construction. A local plasterer was recommended but he proved to be unreliable. He would get drunk and not show up or show up drunk. We finally gave up on the plasterer who was always plastered, and hired a man from Carson City who completed the job for us. Building our own house was a wonderful experience and the final product proved to be a comfortable place we loved. As our family grew, we added rooms to the house: a master bedroom suite, a fourth bedroom, a large living room, a glassed in porch, and a large fireplace. I hand picked the used bricks in Reno and we hauled them to Hawthorne.

We raised two children in Hawthorne. James was born in 1943 and Linda followed in 1945. We didn't have the worries or concerns of parents today. The community was safe and crime was almost non-existent. We never locked the house, in fact, I don't remember having a key. I did most of the Mom things with my kids. I was a den mother for Jim's Cub Scout group and a leader for Linda's Brownies. Children played out of doors, walked to their friends' homes and to school.

Being close to Walker Lake was a plus for our family. Floyd found a ski boat he wanted to buy. It was in Texas, but he bought it and had it shipped to Hawthorne. Boating on Walker Lake became our family's main summer activity. The navy had upgraded Walker Lake, building boat ramps and piers, and improving the beaches at various points around the lake. It became a first-class recreational boating area, thanks to the Navy. We would often arrive at ten o'clock in the morning and return home late in the evening, spending the entire day on the beach and lake. We would eat lunch on the beach, water ski all day, and have a barbeque for dinner. As a result, Jim and Linda became excellent water skiers, a bit ironic, considering we were in the middle of the Nevada desert.

After Linda and Jim started school, I taught full time for nineteen years in Hawthorne. I taught fifth and sixth grades at first, and later mathematics and science in the seventh and eight grades.

I learned to drive a school bus so I could take the students on field trips and not be bound by limitations of carpooling. Bus drivers are required to have a chauffeur's license to transport passengers. Driving the bus was not difficult; parking was the problem. When it came time for the driving test, I was the only teacher; the other applicants were senior high school students. I was the only one who passed because I could park the bus. When the students learned that they had failed the test and I had passed, they looked puzzled. What they didn't know was, that, as a teacher, I had access to the bus parking lot where I practiced after school, but most of them got their licenses on the second or third attempt.

Having a chauffeur's license was helpful later when I belonged to the F.H.A., "Future Homemakers of America." The local organization had a membership of 25 and we often attended meetings in Tonapah and Fallon. I became the designated bus driver. One year we went to Elko to a F.H.A. convention for three days and I drove our group on one of the Hawthorne District School buses. I couldn't help but think how far I had progressed since driving Grandmother May to Sacramento when I was just twelve years old.

HAWTHORNE'S GOLF COURSE

When we arrived in Hawthorne in 1941, there was no golf course or any plan to build one. Floyd loved the game and was so desperate to play that when we lived in Wells he and his principal constructed a putting green for practice on weekends. The putting green was actually black. They leveled an area in the sand and poured oil and tar to make a smooth surface so they could practice putting.

As the population of Hawthorne increased, many of the new arrivals, both civilian and military, had an interest in golf. A group of golfers, frustrated that they had no place to play, came together in hopes of promoting a course. There were thirty-five participants who each donated $30.00 to start exploring the possibility of building a community course. We discovered that the base commander was a golfer and he was also interested in our venture, which became a windfall for the project. Our plan was to build a three-hole course. His interest was probably from a public relations and community development perspective, however, he proved to be very helpful to our project and provided land on the Navy base on which to build a course. The community golf course committee started to clear the land and attempted to construct the course themselves. We were not making much progress because none of us knew what we were doing. Just about the time we were getting discouraged, a wonderful thing happened. The government assigned a unit of the Seabees (Navy's Construction Battalion, thus the name CB) to Hawthorne. The Seabees consisted of carpenters, bricklayers, and building engineers with vast experience in construction. As the war progressed they carved airfields in the jungles of New Guinea and Tarawa and built huge quonset huts and sewer systems on the islands of the Pacific. A golf course in Hawthorne was an easy job. I think they felt sorry for us when they saw our feeble attempt at building the course, so they moved in and took over the project on their own time.

Shortly after the golf course was completed, a new captain was assigned as base commander. Apparently, he didn't approve of a civilian-military partnership so he refunded all the money we had donated toward the project. We all got our $30.00 back. He wanted the golf course to be a military project and soon expanded it to nine holes, which was not only available to military personnel, but also to the community at large. It is currently the only golf course in Hawthorne.

I learned to play golf on this course. I never had a lesson, just learned to hit the ball, and with a little coaching from Floyd and friends, I became a pretty good golfer. I loved the game and it soon became a passion. Because of our little project in Hawthorne, I have had the privilege of playing some of the most beautiful courses in the American West.

RETIREMENT

After 28 years in Hawthorne, Floyd decided to retire. We were proud of his accomplishments and the expansion of the school district during his tenure. We stayed in Hawthorne an additional year after his retirement so I could continue teaching. However, after completing that year, I resigned after 19 years as a teacher in Hawthorne and we moved to Reno. We had some mixed emotions about leaving. Our children had been born there, we pursued our careers there, witnessed massive community growth during the war years and made lifelong friends. We never regretted the decision to settle in this little central Nevada town, but felt it was time to move on and we wanted to return to Reno.

We bought a home in Reno and I taught at Mamie Towles Grammar School for nine more years. Floyd occupied himself with a variety of projects. He drove a school bus for special trips, but that endeavor was short lived because he felt uncomfortable with the responsibility of transporting students. Because he was active in the Lions' Club, he turned his energies to organizing a paper-recycling program. Special bins were placed in strategic positions around Reno where people could deposit their old newspapers and magazines. The garbage department collected the paper, sold it to a recycler and reimbursed the Lions' Club for its efforts. In addition Floyd was hired to run the Northern Nevada Safety Council, which provided driving instruction for individuals who had lost their licenses or had traffic violations.

After I retired from teaching, I reflected on the hundreds of students I had taught over the years. I remember the troublemakers, but they were a minority. Most of the students were good kids and I am fond of many of them. One of my students, Jerry Hall, developed the transportation system providing bus service for the first time in Reno. Pattie Priest, who was a sixth grade student at Mamie Towles, was an outstanding girl who chose a career in computer technology in Silicon valley and was later recruited by Bill Gates and now works in Seattle for Microsoft. Pattie visited me recently and updated me on her life and career. It is rewarding to realize that the product of your labor is reflected in the young people who achieve success and happiness in their chosen vocations.

After my retirement our lives consisted of golf during the day, and bridge and pinochle at night. My cousin and her husband owned an airplane. The four of us would fly to Palm Springs each year and play golf every day. The game became a passion with both of us and every golf course became a challenge and a new experience. We also played some wonderful courses in the Arizona desert. It was fascinating to see the lush green golf courses tucked between the sandy hills and scrub brush of the surrounding arid landscape.

Our daughter Linda was teaching on a military base in Belgium, which provided us an opportunity for our first trip to Europe. After one year, she was transferred to the Netherlands and stationed in Brunssum, Holland, so we packed our suitcases once more and embarked on our second trip to "the continent." This time we lived with Linda in an apartment. It just happened to be the tallest building in town from which we enjoyed marvelous views of the city and countryside.

We cruised the Panama Canal with Henry and Ethel Gilbert, our friends from Hawthorne, who owned the dry goods store there. Because they were interested in everything and never complained about anything, they made great traveling companions. It was a sobering experience for this former teacher to witness the operation of the locks, which I had attempted to explain to my geography classes during my years of teaching.

We took some other trips with the Gilberts, a ten day vacation in Maui, and a memorable trip to Spain. In Spain, we first took a guided tour with a teachers' group, then, extended our stay ten days and rented an apartment on the Costa del Sol. After the tour group departed, the four of us did some additional sightseeing, traveling as far as Gibraltar.

One day we needed some groceries so we could prepare breakfast in our apartment. Floyd and Hank volunteered to go to the market, so we ladies reluctantly accepted their offer. There was milk on the shopping list, but they couldn't find any in the store's refrigerators. Finally, they found a clerk who could speak English and he pointed out the fresh milk which was sitting on the shelves. They expressed some skepticism that unrefrigerated milk could be very fresh but the clerk assured them, "If there's any left at the end of the day, then we put it in the refrigerator."

One of the most amusing experiences was watching Hank Gilbert on the beach in Spain. Just outside our apartment window, there were hundreds of ladies sunning themselves, all topless. There were little girls with sprouting buds and old ladies with droopy mammaries, and everything in between. Hank couldn't handle it. He tried not to look but it was impossible. Everywhere we walked there were women with their breasts exposed. Hank would cast his eyes downward or gaze upward and sometimes even walk in circles to avoid confrontation. He compensated by giggling. Floyd and I adjusted after the initial shock, but poor Hank never conquered his aversion to nudity.

Our happiest days were about to end, however. In November, 1993, Floyd was not feeling well and was trying everything to avoid seeing the doctor. Finally, he went in for an examination and three days before Thanksgiving we were told that Floyd had stomach and pancreatic cancer and would probably not live until Christmas. It was a devastating blow to our family and me, but we appreciated the doctor's frankness.

Floyd did not make it until Christmas. He died in our home December 22nd, three days before Christmas, in 1993. He didn't suffer much and for that I am thankful. Hospice came to our home and helped us during the last days. I lost my life's love, my best friend, my soul mate, and partner in my life's greatest adventures. We had been married 56 years and were never really separated for any length of time. We did everything together, playing golf, building houses, teaching, and traveling the world. When Floyd died, I knew my life was changed forever. I was on my own for the first time since 1937 when we stood before Monsignor Wientjes in Carson City and became man and wife. Losing Floyd was a sobering reality, but I realized I still had my children, my grandchildren and my friends. No one could ever take Floyd's place, but somehow, I'd have to find a way to keep living.

MY FRIEND WILMA

Wilma Birks is one of my oldest and dearest friends. Her family had been helpful and supportive of Floyd during his childhood and early adult years. Wilma's grandparents, the Zenis, and the Smalley family were neighbors in Reno. Wilma's grandmother bought Floyd his first suit so he could attend the University of Nevada. In addition, Wilma's mother, Angelina Birks, helped Floyd financially after he started the university.

When Floyd and I began dating during my freshman year at college, the Birkses and Zenis seemed like part of my extended family. Wilma's mother, Angelina, was a school teacher in Reno for many years. In addition to teaching grammar school, she taught naturalization classes to immigrants seeking American citizenship. As part of this endeavor, and because she spoke Italian, many of the immigrants sought her counsel and advice on a variety of problems and legal matters. She was generous with her time and helped scores of people who needed assistance and guidance in matters they did not understand. She would frequently appear in court with them to resolve legal situations.

When I first met Wilma she was ten years old and I was eighteen, and she seemed like a little girl to me. When we were together at the Smalley home, Angelina would ask Wilma to play the piano. Even though she was very accomplished, she was terribly shy and reluctant to perform, but her mother would insist and she would eventually honor us with a song or two.

After Wilma received her teaching credential in 1946, Floyd offered her a job to teach second grade in Hawthorne where he was principal of the grammar school at the time. Wilma accepted the position and moved to Hawthorne where she taught for fifteen years. She often commented, "Hawthorne was a wonderful place to teach. The school system created the environment and provided the resources a teacher needed to do the job. Why would I want to go anyplace else?"

Wilma and I have had some adventures together. After we both retired, we were invited to Tropic, Utah by Lamar La Fever, another former principal from Hawthorne. After his retirement, he opened a Bed and Breakfast in Tropic, a small town near Bryce Canyon National Park. He promised us he would provide a tour through the park in addition to lodging and meals at the Bed and Breakfast. We accepted his invitation and decided to drive from Reno to Tropic.

I had recently purchased a new Oldsmobile from the dealership in Carson City. The car seemed fine until we got to Fallon. We discovered that something was wrong with the transmission because the car would not back up. We were not going to start across Nevada on US Highway 50, "The Loneliest Highway in America," with a defective auto, so we drove around Fallon looking for an Oldsmobile dealership. There was no such thing so we settled for a Ford agency. We drove in and explained our situation to the manager who was most helpful to two distressed women. He called the Carson City

Oldsmobile agency and explained our problem. They agreed to hire a tow truck and return the car to Carson City and suggested we rent a car and continue our trip to Bryce Canyon.

The Ford agency in Fallon also rented cars so we rented a Ford, a car neither of us had ever driven. The first problem was that Wilma could not figure out how to adjust the seat so she could reach the pedals. We worked and twisted all the levers but nothing happened. During our efforts to adjust the seats the tow truck arrived. Wilma got out of the Ford, approached the driver and said, "Sir, do you have any idea how to adjust this seat so I can reach the pedals?"

He looked at Wilma, said, "Yes," and solved our problem instantly. We left Fallon proceeding east on Highway 50 toward Utah when the second problem arose: it started to rain. Wilma was driving so she took the left side of the dashboard and I took the right, turning every knob and pushing every button, attempting to engage the windshield wipers. Blowers came on, fresh air circulated, the radio blasted country music, and blinkers flashed before one of us hit the right switch and we were once again able to see the road. As with most desert showers, this one passed quickly. By this time we were familiar with the location of the wiper button and were able to turn them off.

About this time Wilma said, "Elma, it's going to get dark soon. Do you know where the light switch is located?"

"No, I have no idea." I opened the glove compartment and fortunately found the owner's manual. As we advanced down the highway into darkness, I was reading all the statistics and features of the Ford including how to change the oil, fuel consumption, recommended tire pressures and safety features. Finally, I found a dashboard diagram and located the light switch. We both felt that we had the Ford mastered and continued east on the lonely highway. The moral of this story is, "If in doubt, read the instructions."

After this rocky start, our trip was wonderful. We arrived at the Bed and Breakfast in Tropic and Lamar treated us like princesses. The accommodations were outstanding and his personal tour through the park was most rewarding.

The return trip was uneventful now that we knew how the Ford worked. We drove to Fallon and the manager of the Ford agency told us to keep the car a couple more days until we could get to Carson City and pick up the Oldsmobile. We drove on to Reno and the following day went to Carson to re-claim the Olds that would now back up. From Carson City we drove the two cars to Fallon, dropped off the Ford, thanked the manager for all his courtesy and assistance, and returned to Reno, ending an adventurous trip.

Wilma is always there for me when I need transportation to the doctor's office or some other appointment. After I developed arthritis and degeneration in my knees, it was difficult for me to drive, but my friend called me almost every day and was available to assist me in whatever I needed. I am grateful for her consideration and loyalty during those difficult times and treasure her friendship.

LOOKING DOWN
THE ROAD

A friend asked me recently, "Don't you ever complain about anything?" My answer was, "No, I have nothing to complain about." I feel fortunate to have lived the life I've lived and experienced the joys I've experienced. I have friends who complain about everything—medical problems, aches and pains, where they live, the weather, etc. I have never been bored or unhappy. I just don't have time. My body is generally pretty good and I can still remember most things. My hips and knees have failed me and I'm not a candidate for replacements so I use a wheelchair to get around. This limits my activities, but I still play bridge and go out to dinners and lunches. I even traveled to Hawaii and found that I could go anyplace on Oahu because every place has handicap access. The wheelchair is only a minor inconvenience. It's one's attitude and state of mind that are important. I wheeled around the entire Aloha stadium flea market in Honolulu on a Sunday afternoon. It's easy to say, "I'm disabled and I can't do that." That's not my style. I want to do things, see things, experience things and live life to the fullest. If my hips and knees worked the way they should, I would be home only long enough to do the laundry and repack my suitcase for the next trip. I've seen a lot in this world, but there are many more places I'd like to visit.

My children are considerate and helpful. Linda lives in Colorado Springs and visits me frequently. Jim lives nearby and takes me to dinner every Sunday. I see grand-children and friends and keep busy. When I look back at the experiences and joys I've had in my life, how could I possibly complain or be discontented? After all, I stared out in a boxcar and now live in a beautiful condominium with indoor plumbing. But most of all, I thank God for His greatest gift–Floyd.

"ELMA-BORN IN A BOXCAR"

by
Gene O'Briant
cover by
Robert Fontana

A book of vignettes about
Elma Smalley
just in time for her
90th Birthday

Please come to a
Book Signing Birthday Bash

Saturday, February 25th
Open House - One to Five o'clock
2940 Deer Run Drive
Reno, Nevada

RSVP 775-825-0902   No gifts, please

Printed in the United States
43918LVS00001B/100-111